The Night He Was Betrayed

The Night He Was Betrayed

"Moving and profoundly insightful. Brad Goad's beautiful telling of the night Jesus was betrayed covers me with chills and fills my eyes with tears. Readers will be thrilled by this wonder-filled book of truth that sets them free. *The Night He Was Betrayed* is a celebration of God's truth and love!"

—**RAGAN COURTNEY,** Author of the musicals *Celebrate Life* and *Bright, New Wings*, Former Professor at Southern Baptist Seminary and Houston Baptist University

"Step by step, hour by hour, and at times, word for word through the final hours of Christ's life, *The Night He Was Betrayed* devotional prepares readers to experience Easter in a fresh and meaningful way. Brad Goad proves to be a skillful Bible teacher, encouraging readers to ponder the significance of Jesus's journey toward the cross. He offers dynamic insights into various relationships that marked the life of our Lord. A fantastic discipleship resource!"

—**MARIAN JORDAN ELLIS,** Author of *For His Glory: Living as God's Masterpiece, A Study of Ephesians*, Host of the *This Redeemed Life* podcast

"Brad uses his God-given gift of creativity to bring this important night to life while helping us experience the Easter season in a much more meaningful way. I heard it said once that the Lord is always better than He has to be. This book will prepare your heart to expect His goodness not only in this story but in your day-to-day life."

—**FAITH WHATLEY,** Former Director of Adult Ministry, LifeWay Christian Resources

"Brad Goad does a masterful job giving the reader a fresh look at a very familiar topic. In each chapter, he describes the intimate details that most Christians never see. Readers are carried through thoughtful and profound narratives that leave them excited to continue to the next chapter. Brad provides us a pre-Easter Bible study that helps 'fill the gap' that many of us feel."

—**DR. RANDY GINNAN,** Regional President, Apartment Life

The Night He Was Betrayed

Jesus, 12 Disciples, and
Life-Changing Lessons from
the Upper Room

BRAD GOAD

R8 MINISTRIES • HOUSTON, TEXAS

Easter Devotional Series
THE NIGHT HE WAS BETRAYED
Jesus, 12 Disciples, and Life-Changing Lessons from the Upper Room

© 2022 Brad Goad
Published by R8 Ministries

For information, contact:
Brad Goad
R8 Ministries
bradgoad@gmail.com

Paperback ISBN: 979-8-9856535-0-2
E-book ISBN: 979-8-9856535-1-9

READ ALL THREE BOOKS
IN THE EASTER DEVOTIONAL SERIES:

To Rainy, the love of my life.

*Her creative spirit motivates me to look
beyond the surface in Scripture and life. She inspires me to be
not only a better man, but more importantly,
a better man of God.*

On the Night He Was Betrayed

Matt. 20:25-28, John 13:1-17, Eph.5:21, Phil. 2:1-11

On the night he was betrayed

Jesus led them to a feast

And invited everyone

Even Judas had a seat

And he showed them how the bread

Must be broken first before they could be fed

And he poured the wine to say

How much he loved them

On the night he was betrayed

On the night he was betrayed

Jesus knelt before the feet

They would use to run away

And washed them clean

When they could not believe it

He said, "You must to able to receive it"

And so, their king became their slave

And he served them

On the night he was betrayed

On the night he was betrayed

Jesus led them in a song

To a God who will not change

No matter how far we go wrong

And he said that in the end

They'd forsake him, but he never would give up
on them

And he kept the vow he made

And he's kept it since the night he was betrayed

And he kept the vow he made

And he's kept it since the night he was betrayed

By Kyle Matthews, "On The Night He Was Betrayed," created January 28, 2000, Track 4 on *Sing Down*, BMG Songs, Inc./See for Yourself Music (ASCAP), Digital MP3.

Contents

Preface

In recent years, I've reflected on how we celebrate the two major religious holidays.

We are good at preparing for Christmas. Retail stores help out by decorating in October and starting marketing promotions. Churches spend the entire month of December singing Christmas music and observing Advent.

But Easter is different. Some observe Lent, which is meaningful. Others observe Passion Week with stations of the cross that prompt reflection. But there is not really a prolonged period of time in which to prepare our hearts for Easter in a personal way.

When challenged by my pastor to create programming for the adult ministry in my new position, I immediately wanted to develop a pre-Easter Bible study. It would fulfill a gap in my life and in the lives of the people around me. And I could think of no better place to start than focusing on the night Jesus was betrayed.

I also could think of no better inspiration than the song, "On the Night He was Betrayed." It's written by a friend of mine, Kyle Matthews, a gifted singer-songwriter I met years ago in Nashville. His talent goes beyond the commercial success of songs he writes. He tells stories that enter souls and capture hearts. My favorite songs of his seem to be those that do not make it onto the radio charts but that connect with me melodically and take me on a journey with the lyrics—none as much as the song, "On the Night He was Betrayed." Its haunting melody invites me into the darkest of nights and transports me into the upper room. I have replayed it time and time again. It is a song I have listened to often throughout the years.

Kyle's lyrics inspired me to ponder the words, thoughts, actions, and meaning of all that took place on the darkest of nights. Thus, I stepped into the Gospels and entered the large, furnished room upstairs. I listened to the conversations that were recorded and watched the movements of Jesus that took the disciples by surprise. I wrestled with the lessons that were taught. I was amazed, humbled, and grieved to watch the celebration of the meal unfold—and unravel—right before my eyes.

The Night He Was Betrayed is the journey through that fateful evening. It is a three-week pre-Easter Bible study that was presented live to an adult ministry in the period leading up to Easter. It has now found its way into this book.

My prayer is that the words on these pages will help you prepare your heart for the grandest celebration of all. For you and I to fully appreciate the light of the resurrection, I invite you to walk with me into the darkness of the night Jesus was betrayed.

Acknowledgments

I would like to thank my beautiful bride, Rainy, who has encouraged me every step of the way. She has been here from the very beginning, when I prepared the presentations of the original three-week pre-Easter Bible study. Day by day and year by year, she has challenged, encouraged, and loved me fully and completely.

Thanks to my parents, who have always been supportive of the coexistence of ministry and creativity.

Thanks to seminary professors Ragan Courtney and the late William "Bill" Hendricks, who taught me to look at the creativity of God with fresh eyes and at the character of God's people with an open mind.

Thanks to the 60+ ministry and the staff at Second Baptist Church for their prayers, partnership, and encouragement. A shout out especially to those on the C-Hall who are extraordinary co-laborers for Christ and who know how to make life-changing ministry fun.

Thanks to Rado Javor, the talented artist who created the artwork used on the cover, which invites us into the large, furnished room upstairs.

Finally, thanks to my college friends Steve Williams and Kevin McClean, who have proven that friendship goes beyond time, geography, and technology. Both men have been a constant encouragement on my journey of life.

1

Introduction

Sometimes picking a place to eat can be difficult. There are times when a simple conversation about where to eat turns into a complex discussion of prices, menus, preferences, and wait time.

It usually starts with an unassuming question: "Where do you want to eat?"

When asked by a wife, her husband may respond quickly with, "It doesn't matter." This is not always the best answer for a husband to give his wife, even when it does not really matter.

But unless you are a foodie, it usually does *not* matter the kind of food or even the place. Food is primarily sustenance. It is a necessity that, so as long as the person is able to eat somewhere, is going to be acceptable. No harm, no foul.

There are, however, those occasions when the significance of the moment is such that where you choose to eat *does* matter. The occasion could be a birthday, anniversary, graduation, or holiday celebration. The food matters. The ambiance matters. The lighting matters. The music, or lack thereof, matters.

When those occasions occur, thought goes into the selection of a place to eat. Similar to the law of real estate, it's about location, location, location. For a special, significant, benchmark occasion, the place where you eat not only matters but will also be remembered.

And so it was for thirteen men in a large, furnished room upstairs on the night a celebration turned into a betrayal.

Chapter 1

The Question

T HE NIGHT JESUS was betrayed began with a meal. It
started with a seemingly simple question, "Where do you
want to eat?" But in reality, it was not a simple question.

The answer to the question would set the stage
for a life-changing meal. A life-changing moment. A
life-changing example.

A life-changing lesson.

Matthew recorded it like this:

MATTHEW 26:17-19 *Now on the first day of Unleav-
ened Bread the disciples came to Jesus and asked,
"Where do You want us to prepare for You to eat the
Passover?" And He said, "Go into the city to a certain
man, and say to him, 'The Teacher says, "My time is
near; I am keeping the Passover at your house with
My disciples."' The disciples did as Jesus had directed
them; and they prepared the Passover.*

It was a simple question that had probably been asked or heard countless times over their three years together: "Jesus, where do you want to eat?" The disciples asked a very general question that could have easily been answered, "It doesn't matter."

But it did matter.

Jesus knew it mattered—even when the disciples asking the question did not grasp the weight of their question. This would be the last time all thirteen of them would gather around a table for a meal together. Jesus knew the significance of where they would eat and what would take place in that location.

Now, it had been a long week for all of them, especially for Jesus. A few days earlier, there had been a parade of sorts, a true celebration that had drawn crowds of people lining the streets. Jesus had been very specific in giving directions to His disciples about what He would need for that particular occasion.

It mattered.

Mark described the scenario like this:

MARK 11:1-7 *And as they approached Jerusalem, at Bethphage and Bethany, near the Mount of Olives, He sent two of His disciples, and said to them, "Go into the village opposite you, and immediately as you enter it you will find a colt tied there, on which no one has ever sat; untie it and bring it here. And if anyone says to you, 'Why are you doing this?' say, 'The Lord has need of it'; and immediately he will send it back here." They went away and found a colt tied at the* *door, outside in the street; and they untied it. And some of the bystanders were saying to them, "What are you doing, untying the colt?" And they told them just as Jesus had said, and they gave them permission. They brought the colt to Jesus and put their cloaks on it; and He sat on it.*

The instructions had been carried out accordingly. As a result, there was a grand, spectacular, festive celebration. Palm branches were laid on the ground, providing a symbolic foundation of triumph and victory. Palm Sunday has been carried out for more than two thousand years to commemorate the significance of that moment.

The palm branches perhaps also had been waved as the crowds gathered and shouted with enthusiasm, "Hosanna! Blessed is He Who Comes in the Name of the Lord" (Matthew 21:19). And as the celebration continued, "Blessed is the King, the One who comes in the name of the Lord; Peace in heaven and glory in the highest!" (Luke 19:38).

What a way to start a week. And what a difference a few days can make.

Then the disciples asked, "Where do you want to eat?"

It's not a stretch to think the disciples, at least eleven of them, were excited with anticipation of what this Passover would be like. If the week had started with such a celebration, would it not end in grand style?

No one would have suspected what would occur on the night Jesus would be betrayed.

Chapter 2

The Answer

T HE QUESTION DESERVED an answer that would
show how much the location mattered.

> **LUKE 22:10-13** *And He said to them, "When you
> have entered the city, a man carrying a pitcher
> of water will meet you; follow him into the house
> that he enters. And you shall say to the owner of
> the house, 'The Teacher says to you, "Where is the
> guest room in which I may eat the Passover with My
> disciples?"' And he will show you a large, furnished
> upstairs room; prepare it there." And they left and
> found everything just as He had told them; and they
> prepared the Passover.*

Location, location, location. It has come to be known as
the "upper room." More specifically, it was a large, furnished
room upstairs.

This would be the location of the last time all thirteen of them would be together. This would be the location of the last time they would eat together. It would be the last time they would all talk together, perhaps even laugh together. It would be the last time that each of the twelve disciples would trust the other eleven implicitly.

This would be the location where everything would begin to change. This would be the location where there was no turning back, the point of no return.

The location mattered.

This room was not a main thoroughfare. It was not in the main part of the house. It was not centralized, which prevented disturbances or interruptions. It was secluded. In the first century, the rooms located on a second floor would have stairs primarily on the outside of the house, providing a private entrance.

The week had started with such grandeur and celebration. But now, there were no people lining the streets. There were no palm branches being laid down or even waved. No one was shouting praise and honor, and no crowds were gathered. It was no longer a celebration for all to see.

It was a meal with thirteen men who had traveled together, fished together, laughed together, and lived life together for more than three years. It was a meal that would be their last together. And it would take place in a large, private, furnished room upstairs on the night Jesus would be betrayed.

Chapter 3

The Hour

JESUS KNEW THIS moment was coming. The clock was ticking from the moment of His first breath as a newborn baby in Bethlehem thirty-three years earlier. The clock of history was counting down, and His hour had come.

John recorded it like this:

> **JOHN 13:1** *Now before the Feast of the Passover, Jesus, knowing that His hour had come that He would depart out of this world to the Father, having loved His own who were in the world, He loved them to the end.*

Jesus knew what the other twelve in the large, furnished room upstairs did not know: His hour had come. The Greek word is *hora*, which means a specific, literal time. Solomon would write:

ECCLESIASTES 3:1-2A *There is an appointed time for everything. And there is a time for every matter under heaven—a time to give birth and a time to die.*

There was a time under the rule of King Herod when Caesar Augustus ordered a census for everyone to register in their own cities. Joseph and Mary would have to travel to Bethlehem while Mary was "great with child." It was time for heaven to come down to earth and for people to see God in the flesh. It was time for Mary to give birth in a stable behind a crowded inn, located in an unassuming little town called Bethlehem. It was time for history to change.

Fast forward thirty-three years, and now the hour had come for Jesus to have His last meal with His twelve chosen disciples. These were men whom He had asked to follow Him, none of them knowing where He would lead.

None had known that Jesus would lead them to a side of the mountain overlooking the sea of Galilee and preach a sermon on how to live life. And none had known that Jesus would lead them beyond the region of Galilee, to Caesarea Philippi, where Simon would become Peter, the rock. They hadn't expected that Jesus would lead them through Samaria and have a conversation with a woman by a well. And they hadn't expected that Jesus would lead them to Jerusalem on more than one occasion, though none of the occasions with the kind of reception they had experienced just a few days before He had led them to this large furnished, room upstairs.

After all the miles traveled and villages visited, and after all the encounters with the Pharisees and Sadducees, His hour had come. His hour had come after all the teachings in the synagogues, hillsides, boats, and homes, and after all the healings and miracles, and after the triumphal entry and cleansing of the temple. His hour had come in this large, furnished room upstairs.

The time had come for the Passover meal on the night Jesus was betrayed.

The Passover

THE PASSOVER MEAL was nothing new for Jesus and the disciples. This was something they had celebrated annually their entire lives. Their parents and grandparents—and generations long before them—had celebrated this meal. It had been observed annually this time of year since the days of Moses.

For the Jews, Passover was an appointed time to reflect, remember, and celebrate what God had done for His children when in Egypt. And it took place in the darkness of the night.

God's people had been in bondage as slave workers in Egypt for over four hundred years. Generation after generation, the Hebrew people had experienced no life other than that of slaves working in Egypt. They had not rebelled against the pharaohs over their hundreds of years of rule. They had developed a work ethic during this time that would serve them well. This was the life they had grown to know and accept. But it was during these four hundred years that God's people were fruitful and multiplied. They had grown in number over the generations.

Because the Hebrew people had multiplied in number so greatly, one pharaoh ordered all newborn baby boys to be thrown in the Nile to be drowned. Most were, though one was not drowned. When his Hebrew mother could no longer hide the baby boy after three months, she put him in a papyrus basket, covered it with tar and pitch, and gently placed the basket in the Nile.

In God's sovereignty, the daughter of Pharaoh found the basket with the baby boy inside. She allowed the birth mother to continue to nurse the baby and still receive wages. The baby was named Moses because he was drawn out of the water, and Moses was raised in the household of Pharaoh. He was educated as an Egyptian. He was respected as an Egyptian. He was a leader within the realm of Egypt. This was the life of Moses for forty years.

Then everything changed.

At the approximate age of forty, Moses witnessed an Egyptian beating a Hebrew. Seeing no one else was around, Moses ended up killing the Egyptian and literally fled for his life, escaping Egypt with no desire to return. He carved out a new life as a shepherd, got married, had kids, and was a family man. This was the life of Moses for his next forty years.

Then everything changed again.

At the age of eighty, God had other plans for Moses. As described in Exodus 3, Moses was called by God through a burning bush that would not be consumed. God would use

Moses and his brother Aaron to lead the Hebrew people, the children of God, out of Egypt to a land of promise.

The time had come for God's people to be freed from bondage in Egypt. The time had come for freedom, yet Pharaoh refused to let God's people go. Through nine plagues, the heart of Pharaoh grew harder and harder. After each plague, Pharaoh continued to answer "no" to God's request. He refused time and time again. Thus came the tenth and final plague.

> **EXODUS 11:1** *Now the Lord said to Moses, "One more plague I will bring on Pharaoh and on Egypt; after that he will let you go from here. When he lets you go, he will assuredly drive you out from here completely.*

The previous plagues were gruesome and grotesque in their own rights, but all of them were indirect in nature. None of them hit home, so to speak. None of them were personal to the Pharaoh until the tenth and final plague.

> **EXODUS 11:4-5** *Then Moses said, "This is what the Lord says: 'About midnight I am going out into the midst of Egypt, and all the firstborn in the land of Egypt shall die, from the firstborn of the Pharaoh who sits on his throne, to the firstborn of the slave girl who is behind the millstones; all the firstborn of the cattle as well.'"*

This time, it was personal.

God was going to carry out this plague in dramatic fashion as judgment. Yet as always is the case, God's judgment comes with an option of grace, a way of escape. It is the grace of God found in the Passover.

The instructions were seemingly cruel but clear.

EXODUS 12:1-7 *Now the Lord said to Moses and Aaron in the land of Egypt, "This month shall be the beginning of months for you; it is to be the first month of the year for you. Speak to all the congregation of Israel, saying, 'On the tenth of this month they are, each one, to take a lamb for themselves, according to the fathers' households, a lamb for each household. Now if the household is too small for a lamb, then he and his neighbor nearest to his house are to take one according to the number of persons in them; in proportion to what each one should eat, you are to divide the lamb. Your lamb shall be an unblemished male a year old; you may take it from the sheep or from the goats. You shall keep it until the fourteenth day of the same month, then the whole assembly of the congregation of Israel is to slaughter it at twilight. Moreover, they shall take some of the blood and put it on the two doorposts and on the lintel of the houses in which they eat it.'"*

The grace of God comes with a price and a step of action. The action is two-fold. God has His part, and the people have their part. Interesting to note: this all took place at night.

EXODUS 12:12-14 *"For I will go through the land of Egypt on that night, and fatally strike all the firstborn* *in the land of Egypt, from the human firstborn to animals; and against all the gods of Egypt I will execute judgments—I am the Lord. The blood shall be a sign for you on the houses where you live; and when I see the blood I will **pass over** you, and no plague will come upon you to destroy you when I strike the land of Egypt. Now this day shall be a memorial to you, and you shall celebrate it as a feast to the Lord; throughout your generations you are to celebrate it as a permanent ordinance."*

All the Jewish generations since the days of Moses had commemorated the Passover. It was a symbol of God's protection and provision. It was a way to show thankfulness to God for the freedom He provides. It was a way to remember that there is bondage in life that can hold us back when we refuse to move forward in faith. It was a way to celebrate a new life when we are willing to take that first step of trusting God at His word.

The Passover would always be a time to reflect, remember, and celebrate. It was nothing new for Jesus and the twelve disciples who would be celebrating this occasion in a large, furnished room upstairs on the night Jesus was betrayed.

— *Chapter 5* —

The Conversation

YOU WOULD EXPECT that the disciples' meal would be a reverent time together commemorating the Passover around a table. You would perhaps expect a time of silence and prayer. Perhaps a time of reading Hebrew Scripture and giving thanks for specific things God has done over the years.

But the conversation around the table was not exactly what you might expect.

Luke, a physician by trade, gives details about the gathering that other authors may fast-forward through. In this particular case, Luke shows how these thirteen men had become family. Though there were two sets of biological brothers in the midst of the twelve, all of them had become a band of spiritual brothers.

And as is often the case, when "family" gathers around a holiday meal, there are discussions that take place that cause tension or uneasiness. There are voices that grow a bit louder and tones that become a bit more deliberate. There are words used that could be described as condescending rather than encouraging. It is part of being family—and the spiritual band of the disciples was no different.

Luke described the scene like this:

LUKE 22:24 *And a dispute also developed among them as to which one of them was regarded as being the greatest.*

Gathered in this large, furnished room upstairs to commemorate and celebrate the Passover, the discussion became heated. A dispute developed among them. To fully appreciate the scene, we need to understand the words Luke uses, which are not by accident but with inspiration and intent.

+ "Dispute" is the Greek word *philoneikia*, which means "the love of strife; eagerness to contend; rivalry." This is the only time in the New Testament this word is used—again, not by accident.

+ "Developed" is the Greek word *ginomai*, which means "to become; come into existence."

Out of nowhere emerged this "love of strife, rivalry, and eagerness to contend." There is no indication of what brought about this dispute on the night Jesus was betrayed.

But you can imagine the personalities around the table. There were James and John, the "Sons of Thunder," who in a previous incident had asked if they could sit on the right and left of Jesus in Glory (Mark 10:35-45). There was Peter, who often was a loose cannon talking without a filter. And there was Simon the Zealot, a member of a Jewish sect known for standing up strongly for what they believe, with a willingness to use aggression.

These were personalities of twelve men who had traveled miles together over the years and had seen things up close and personal that would make other people shudder in both fear and faith. But now, around this table, all of a sudden and out of nowhere, sprang an argument about who would be the greatest. And with this context about the dispute, we can understand how John developed the next moments around the table on the night Jesus was betrayed.

— *Chapter 6* —

The Devil and the Servant

THERE WAS OBVIOUS tension in the large, furnished room upstairs. It was not the warm, fuzzy feeling portrayed by artists over the centuries. There was a darkness and grittiness to it that we may not want to acknowledge—but was nevertheless real.

Notice how John developed the events of the evening:

JOHN 13:2 *And during supper, the devil having already put into the heart of Judas Iscariot, the son of Simon, to betray Him.*

We tend to focus on the thirteen men who had become family over the previous three years of traveling and ministering together. We tend to focus on the elements of the meal, the bread, and the wine. We tend to focus on the words of Jesus, both of comfort and of challenge.

And we tend to forget the presence of the devil in the room.

We often forget the presence of the devil in any room. But his presence was felt and made an impact on the night Jesus was betrayed. Though Judas was present in body, he had already emotionally left the building. His decision had been made. And unbeknownst to the other eleven disciples, they, too, would be betrayed by one who had been one of them.

John continued the developing story:

JOHN 13:3-4 *Jesus, knowing that the Father had handed all things over to Him, and that He had come forth from God and was going back to God, got up from supper and laid His outer garments aside; and He took a towel and tied it around Himself.*

Consider the setting. The meal in the large, furnished room upstairs was in progress. The devil had already prompted Judas. A dispute had arisen out of nowhere about who would be greatest. It was not the nice, warm, commemorative dinner that one might expect to reflect, remember, and celebrate the Passover from the days of Moses. It was gritty and messy.

But notice what did not happen in this setting. Jesus did not condemn them. He did not dismiss, reject, or shame them. He did not leave them.

On the night He was betrayed, Jesus served them.

He got up from the table. More than likely, He had been lying on the ground, as was customary in that day and culture.

He then took off His outer clothing, a long tunic that men wore that reached down to their shins, just above their ankles. Covering the tunic was a vest of sorts, sometimes of the same length. It was the vest that Jesus took off, leaving the tunic on Him. He took a towel and wrapped it around His waist.

None of this was normal or expected.

His actions would have stunned the disciples. Jesus was their leader. But these were actions of a servant, not a leader.

Jesus had been celebrated and revered as a king just a few days earlier while entering Jerusalem riding on a colt. In reflection, that was a dichotomy as well.

Jesus had healed the sick and caused the blind to see, the lame to walk. Jesus had called out to his friend Lazarus who had died and been buried in a tomb four days: "Lazarus, come out!" And Lazarus had walked out of the tomb alive (John 11:43-44).

Jesus was a teacher and preacher. Jesus was a healer and miracle worker. Jesus was a leader among leaders.

But a servant?

Years later, Paul would reflect on this question. He answered like this:

PHILIPPIANS 2:5-7 *Have this attitude in yourselves which was also in Christ Jesus, who, as He already existed in the form of God, did not consider equality with God something to be grasped, but emptied Himself by **taking the form of a bond-servant** and being born in the likeness of men.*

On the night Jesus was betrayed, Jesus did the unexpected. He became a servant to those who had served Him.

— *Chapter 7* —

The Hands of the Servant

IN THE LARGE, furnished room upstairs, gathered with His twelve disciples, Jesus took a towel and wrapped it around His waist. And then the unthinkable happened.

> **JOHN 13:5** *Then He poured water into the basin, and began washing the disciples' feet and wiping them with the towel which He had tied around Himself.*

If they had been in another house with other people, this could not have happened. More than likely, they would have been in a main thoroughfare of the house, where their feet would have already been washed by a slave or servant, which was customary at the time in that culture.

But remember that Jesus had been specific on the location of this last meal they would have together. He had selected this large, secluded, furnished room upstairs to commemorate the Passover.

The disciples had already proven that evening that they still did not fully understand their role as disciples. They had disputed among themselves who would be the greatest. Yet the One in the room who was truly the greatest among them was now their servant. This was a lesson Jesus had already taught them when He said He had "not come to be served, but to serve, and to give His life as a ransom for many" (Matthew 20:28).

Jesus knew what they did not know or understand: His hour had come. On this night, He would be betrayed by someone in the room. Someone sitting with Him around the table. Someone with dirty feet.

It was time for one more lesson. Without saying the words, Jesus commanded the attention of the disciples to "watch and learn."

Can you imagine their faces when He got up? Food was being eaten, drinks were being poured, and plates were being passed. While the meal was in progress, their leader got up from the table.

Their eyes would have followed Him as He got up. They would have followed Him as He walked over to the side of the room, took off His outer garment, and laid it down. Perhaps their eyes shifted toward one another in doubt and disbelief at what their eyes were seeing. Perhaps they shrugged their shoulders in silence, not understanding what was happening.

When their eyes looked back over at Jesus, He would have had a towel in His hands. The disciples must have wondered, "What does He want with a towel?"

As they stared in disbelief, He took the towel and wrapped it around His waist. A leader did not do that. A teacher or a rabbi did not do that. A healer and miracle worker did not do that. A servant did that!

Jesus bent down and got a basin of water. And then the unthinkable happened. Jesus proceeded toward them as the meal was in progress, as they were still lying at the table.

There was no other possible posture Jesus could have taken other than kneeling down. On the night He was betrayed, it was no other posture than that of a servant.

Jesus grasped the basin of water and moved it closer. He would need easy access to the water so that His hands could lower the towel into the basin.

These were the hands that had gathered the children together (Mark 10:15-16). These hands had touched the untouchables and healed the lepers (Matthew 8:1-3). They had held the mane of the donkey riding triumphantly just a few days ago.

Within a few minutes, these hands would break the bread and pass the wine one last time. Within several hours, these hands would carry a cross. And within a few more hours still, these hands would be nailed to the cross.

These were the same hands that grasped the basin of water, moved it closer to the table, and held the feet of each disciple. Twelve disciples, two feet each. A total of twenty-four feet would be washed the night Jesus was betrayed. They would be washed by the hands of Jesus Himself, the Servant to all.

Chapter 8

The Feet of the Served

O N THE NIGHT He was betrayed, Jesus washed the feet of each disciple, one by one. Each different and unique. Each accepting the invitation of Jesus to follow Him. Each willing to give up everything to follow Jesus.

Well, almost.

Perhaps Jesus had begun with the feet of Philip. After all, Philip had been the first to say yes when Jesus asked if he would follow Him.

As Jesus wiped the heels of the feet of his first follower, He might have remembered testing Philip on the side of a mountain a year or two earlier, near the time of Passover. Seeing a crowd of more than five thousand men plus women and children on the hillside, Jesus had asked Philip how they could feed all those people who were so hungry.

As Jesus held Philip's heels, He might have recalled Philip's response: "It would take more than half a year's wages to buy enough bread for each one to have a bite!" (John 6:7).

Jesus may have had a small smile on His face as He dried the feet of Philip, remembering the miracle fondly. Then Jesus moved on to the feet of Andrew, a good friend of Philip.

As Jesus clutched the wet portion of the towel, perhaps He remembered the same mountainside setting of the miraculous feeding of thousands of people. It was Andrew's feet that had led a young boy who just so happened to have fish and bread loaves to share. Drying the feet of Andrew, Jesus may have beamed, remembering the incredible day that had been shared by all thirteen men.

Jesus scooted over to the next disciple, James the brother of John. As He wet the feet of James, Jesus knew that these feet were going to encounter challenging roads in the days and years ahead. He knew that these feet belonged to the disciple who would be the first to be martyred. He would be martyred for the sake of the One washing his feet now. Though we are not told, perhaps a tear crossed Jesus's face instead of a smile as He dried James's feet.

John, the brother of James, might have been next. He was one of the "Sons of Thunder" who had asked to sit on the right and left of Jesus. But as Jesus washed the feet of John, His thoughts about the request may have been replaced with thoughts about His own mother. These were the feet of the disciple who would watch over Jesus's mother. Mary would soon be in John's care. These feet would take Mary to Ephesus as she lived out her life. Jesus dried the toes of John, knowing that in mere hours He would ask him to do this one thing. It would be asked while Jesus hung on a cross, before taking His last breath.

Bartholomew, also known as Nathaniel, was faithful before accepting the invitation to follow Jesus. As Jesus washed the feet of this disciple, He may have reflected on the fact that Nathaniel was from Cana, the town where it all started. It was in Cana that Jesus turned water into wine at a wedding. With each motion of His hands, Jesus remembered that Nathaniel was always trustworthy, an Israelite indeed in whom there is no deceit (John 1:47).

And then Jesus came to Matthew. These were the feet of a tax collector, one who had worked for the Roman Empire, making money for himself and the hierarchy of the Empire. But these were also the feet of a tax collector who did what few dared: leave it all behind. These feet followed Jesus. As Jesus dried the feet of Matthew, He knew that these feet belonged to the disciple who would write about His genealogy and His first sermon on the side of a mountain.

Among those around the table was one named Thomas, who was never afraid to ask a question. As Jesus lifted up the feet of Thomas, also called Didymus, He washed them carefully with hands that were without blemish, perhaps thinking it would not be long before these hands would look and feel different. These unblemished hands would soon be nail-scarred hands that would be part of the evidence Thomas would require to believe in the grandest of all miracles. But until then, Jesus knew these would be the feet of one who would doubt, at least for a while.

Jesus continued moving the basin from one to the next. There was James the son of Alphaeus, Simon the Zealot, and Judas the son of James. Jesus washed the feet of these three men, knowing they would never be as popular or well known as some of the others in the large, furnished room upstairs. These were the feet of whom some would later refer to as the anonymous disciples.

But the feet of these three men were present with the other nine disciples on the side of the mountain for the first sermon that Jesus preached. The feet of the three men were at the feeding of the five thousand, traveling the same paths as the others. These feet were even at the raising of Lazarus. The feet of these three men were anything but anonymous. They had names, purposes, and a relationship with Jesus. They were willing to follow Him anywhere, just like the others around the table. In fact, the feet of these three followed Jesus when others chose not to.

And then Jesus came to Peter. Peter's feet were the only ones that had been willing to step out of the boat into the middle of the Sea of Galilee. His feet were not afraid to get wet. Initially, however, Peter did not allow Jesus to wash his feet. It seemed improper. Jesus was probably not surprised that it was Peter who pushed back on this process. He explained the situation in a way that helped Peter understand the significance.

As Jesus rubbed Peter's soles—perhaps taking a bit longer, knowing that these feet stood firmly in Caesarea Philippi— Peter proclaimed with great boldness and confidence, "You are the Christ, the Son of the Living God." He likely was pleased that the inner soul of Peter had come to recognize the Messiah. He might have thought about how these feet would run away in bitter shame after denying knowing the One washing his feet in this large, furnished room upstairs. Peter's denial would be another form of betrayal on this fateful night.

Finally, there was Judas, known as Judas Iscariot. Taking the feet of Judas, knowing that Satan had already prompted his heart, Jesus gently and lovingly dripped water over the feet that would walk out of this large, furnished room before anyone else. He rubbed the dirt from between the toes of the man who would soon walk briskly to Roman soldiers with news of where the One washing his feet would be easily found in a garden. Jesus took the towel and dried off the feet of the one who would deceive him later that night with a kiss. Jesus served the one who would betray him.

Jesus finished washing the feet of those who had willingly chosen to follow Him for more than three years throughout Israel. None of them had known where the path would lead, and none of them had any idea where the path down the stairs of the large, furnished room would ultimately take them.

Not even the one who would betray Jesus.

Chapter 9

The Lesson

T HE EVENING HAD begun with a question about where to eat, and now Jesus asked the disciples a question.

JOHN 13:12 *Then, when He had washed their feet, and taken His garments and reclined at the table again, He said to them, "Do you know what I have done for you?"*

This is the question we need to ask ourselves as we prepare for Easter. Do we understand what He has done for us?

If we had been in that large, furnished room upstairs, our feet would have been washed. Jesus washed the feet of those who served Him bravely and faithfully. He washed the feet of those who would take His message to the world beginning in Jerusalem, Judea, Samaria, and to the uttermost parts. He washed the feet of those who would plant churches, write letters and record His genealogy, words, teachings, challenges, and life story.

Jesus washed the feet of those whose names we know well. He also washed the feet of those whose names we rarely remember.

Jesus washed the feet of those who denied Him and of those who doubted Him. He even washed the feet of those who betrayed Him. If we are honest with ourselves, we have denied, doubted, and betrayed the foot washer named Jesus.

When He returned to the table, the meal was still in progress. Jesus asked of them what He asks of us today: "Do you understand what I have done for you?"

When they responded with silence, Jesus proceeded to answer His own question.

JOHN 13:13-17 *You call Me 'Teacher' and 'Lord'; and you are correct, for so I am. So if I, the Lord and the Teacher, washed your feet, you also ought to wash one another's feet. For I gave you an example, so that you also would do just as I did for you. Truly, truly I say to you, a slave is not greater than his master, nor is one who is sent greater than the one who sent him. If you know these things, you are blessed if you do them.*

Jesus was indeed their Lord and Teacher. He was also their Servant. The roles are not mutually exclusive. He was humility personified. And it was just the beginning of how Jesus would serve His disciples in the hours to come.

The example that Jesus set is not one that is comfortable for us today. Whether we wash someone's feet literally or symbolically, it is not easy washing the feet of those who deny us and doubt us. It is a challenge to serve someone who betrays us and hurts us.

Perhaps this season we need to search our hearts. Whom do we need to serve? Not in a public way, with fanfare for all to see, but in a private way, like the large, furnished room upstairs. There may be someone you need to serve, love, and forgive this season. There may be someone whose feet you can wash.

Jesus even made a promise to those who apply His lesson.

JOHN 13:17 *Now that you know these things, you will be* **blessed** *if you do them.*

The word "blessed" had been in the first recorded sermon of Jesus on the side of a mountain. The twelve men in the large, furnished room, now with freshly-washed feet, had been there and had heard His teaching.

MATTHEW 5:3-12 *"Blessed are the poor in spirit, for theirs is the kingdom of heaven.*

"Blessed are those who mourn, for they will be comforted.

"Blessed are the gentle, for they will inherit the earth.

"Blessed are those who hunger and thirst for righteousness, for they will be satisfied.

"Blessed are the merciful, for they will receive mercy.

"Blessed are the pure in heart, for they will see God.

"Blessed are the peacemakers, for they will be called sons of God.

"Blessed are those who have been persecuted for the sake of righteousness, for theirs is the kingdom of heaven.

"Blessed are you when people insult you and persecute you, and falsely say all kinds of evil against you because of Me. Rejoice and be glad, for your reward in heaven is great; for in this same way they persecuted the prophets who were before you."

Now, in the large, furnished room upstairs, Jesus used the word "blessed" again. You will be "blessed" if you do this, He promised. If you put into action the lessons that have been taught, you will be blessed. There is a sense of joy and purpose when you apply the words of Jesus in your life.

It was a sweet and tender moment around that table. It was reflective for most, uncomfortable for one. For there was only one of the twelve who knew it was the night Jesus would be betrayed. There would be a cost that needed to be paid in a matter of hours.

2

The Cost

Introduction

There is always a cost.

Reputation tarnished. Integrity lost. Friendship challenged. Trust broken. Cheek kissed. Arrest made.

Betrayal costs much more than a mere thirty pieces of silver.

The Pharisees and Sadducees had been manipulating and maneuvering in deliberate ways for more than three years, trying to trap Jesus once and for all. Everything they did was anything but fair. There was nothing subtle about the fact that they wanted to denounce the teachings of Jesus. These religious leaders wanted to silence the man named Jesus at any cost.

The Chief Priest, the High Priest, and even Rome itself had been growing increasingly nervous. Jesus was unlike anything or anyone they had ever seen before. It was obvious that Jesus was not going away. It was also obvious His following was growing and intensifying. The attention of the people was being turned from the ways of old, or so it seemed.

The message of Jesus was revolutionary, but He did not seem to be leading a revolt. His followers were ordinary, but together they had extraordinary accomplishments. His personality was gentle and meek, but the stress must have been getting to Him because at the temple just a few days earlier, Jesus had righteous anger like never before when He literally cleansed the temple from being a den of thieves. Tables had turned both literally and figuratively.

And Jesus must have had a whirlwind of thoughts as it was all coming down to this; just a few more hours. In His humanity, not enough time. Surely, it could not end like this. In His divinity, His hour had come, leading to the fulfillment of prophecies foretold.

Just a few more hours to teach those He had been teaching for more than three years. Lessons that began when Jesus offered an individual invitation to twelve nondescript, ordinary, anonymous young men with the words, "Follow Me."

And twelve men did follow Him. They followed Him to the surrounding areas of Galilee. They followed Him to Cana and to Caesarea Philippi. They followed Him to Samaria, which was unheard of for Jews to intentionally visit. They followed Him to Bethany to visit friends Mary, Martha, and Lazarus.

They followed Him to the desert as well as to the water. They followed Him on a boat and on the side of a mountain. They followed Him to the cities and the small, unnamed villages and to the synagogues and temple. They followed Him to Jerusalem. And they followed Him to a large, furnished room upstairs.

Each step they followed came with a cost.

Now, just a few more hours to be together for one more meal, one more laugh. Just a few more hours for one more story, one more lesson, one more challenge. One more prayer. Just a few more hours before the last hymn would be sung together as a group. Just a few more hours before the cost became real, and the price finally paid.

Just a few more hours before everything would change on the night He was betrayed.

Chapter 10

Listening, Watching, Learning

E VERYTHING WAS ABOUT to change.
That was what Jesus told His twelve disciples in the large, furnished room upstairs. They had followed Him faithfully throughout Israel, but life would no longer be like they had known. Relationships would no longer be like they had known. Their faith would no longer be like they had known. Everything would be different, and little did they know it would happen in a matter of hours.

Jesus looked around the room. His disciples were seated around the table after their feet had been washed. Bread had been broken, and wine had been passed. Looking around at the twelve disciples, perhaps He reflected on all the previous lessons that had been taught.

"Have they listened enough?" He may have thought.

"Have they listened to my teachings and words enough? All the times I used Scripture from the Law, Prophets, and Psalms . . . All the teaching in the synagogues, which did not always go well, or on the hillside, which drew more people than we could count. Have they listened enough?

"Have they listened to the parables, the simple word-pictures that gave them heavenly truths? Was Nathaniel listening? Were James and John listening? Was Peter listening? Was Andrew listening? The Pharisees and Sadducees had been listening, and it made them nervous. But have the disciples listened enough?

"Have they watched enough?" He may have pondered.

"Did they notice the simple things, like the times I turned the other cheek? Not always easy, but always right. Did they notice the times I offered a cup of water, sometimes when no one else would?

"Did they notice the times I walked away by Myself to pray and spend time alone with My Father? I loved those times, talking to My Abba. Sometimes not even talking, just sitting in much-needed silence, feeling the gentle wind across My face, the Spirit giving Me comfort. Did they notice I was refreshed each time I came back to them? For three years, have they watched enough?

"Have they learned enough?" He may have wondered.

"Have they learned to trust God when the storms come, when the boat is rocking? Have they learned to forgive those who have done them harm? Have they learned to love those the world has forsaken? Have they learned to pray? Have they learned to depend upon Scripture in their daily lives?

"They have heard questions asked and demands made by the Pharisees. Have they learned not to get distracted by things of the world, even when it is in the guise of religiosity? They have seen the miracles up close and personal. Do they understand it all? Do they understand any of it? After three years, have they learned enough?"

Chapter 11

Remembering the Past

O N THE NIGHT He was betrayed, Jesus prompted the disciples to remember the past while teaching them to prepare for the future. Once again, Luke, the physician, gives us detail and insight into an encounter that the other three Gospel writers do not provide.

> **LUKE 22:35-38** *And He said to them, "When I sent you out without money belt and bag and sandals, you did not lack anything, did you?" They said, "No, nothing." And He said to them, "But now, whoever has a money belt is to take it along, likewise also a bag, and whoever has no sword is to sell his coat and buy one. For I tell you that this which is written must be fulfilled in Me, 'And He was numbered with the transgressors'; for that*

which refers to Me has its fulfillment." They said, "Lord, look, here are two swords." And He said to them, "It is enough."

In the large, furnished room upstairs, Jesus reminds them of the past. Over their three years together, Jesus had sent the disciples out at various times, and each time, He had told them they did not need to take a money belt, traveling bag, or sandals. The ventures could have been long, overnight trips or short, day trips. They could have traveled together as a group or in pairs. Jesus knew they would be taken care of. And, apparently, they had learned that would be the case. It was an act of trust and faith in the provision of God and the kindness of others.

> **LUKE 9:3** *And He said to them, "Take nothing for your journey, neither a staff, nor a bag, nor bread, nor money; and do not even have two tunics apiece."*

He had given these instructions on other occasions as well, and not just to the twelve, but to a group of seventy also. This was to be part of their faith journey in a very practical way. Just as God provided for the birds in the air and flowers in the field, He would provide for them. They had grown accustomed to going out to public places and villages without any worry or concern. Without a sword, moneybag, or coat.

In fact, they had grown accustomed to being welcomed and cared for. But Jesus knew that would not always be the case, as they also had witnessed. He told them that if a particular town or village did not respond favorably, to dust off their feet and move on (Luke 10:1-12). It had become somewhat routine. They had learned the lesson in the past.

In that moment of reminding them of what it used to be like, perhaps Jesus remembered their eyes the first time He told them not to take anything. Their eyes had probably gotten bigger with each word He spoke.

The fishermen of the group must have pushed back in their minds. Perhaps they thought, "We always take extra bait and nets. We always have a bag of snacks. We need to be prepared for any surprises."

The tax collector had to think, "In my former profession, I always had a backup plan. I would always take a little extra money from each person to pad the pot in case Rome became greedier. That way, I wouldn't miss out on what I earned."

The Zealot heard this and probably considered turning around: "We never rely on others! We were trained to overtake others, to plow through and overthrow."

As Jesus reminded them of what it was like in the past, they perhaps reflected on how far they had come in these few years. How they had listened, watched, and learned—and how it shaped their thoughts.

"We don't need extra bait. We have seen Jesus multiply fish and loaves beyond our wildest imaginations."

"We don't need a backup plan. The first plan has always worked without fail, every single time."

"We are not here to overthrow others. We are here to serve and work alongside those around us."

Jesus then asked them if they had ever lacked anything. And the disciples in the large, furnished room upstairs answered without hesitation, "No, nothing." Everything had always worked out, even though there were times of doubt, fear, and seemingly insurmountable odds.

It was like the time they were crossing the Sea of Galilee on the boat at night, and a storm seemed to come out of nowhere. The disciples were terrified, but Jesus remained sleeping. When they woke up Jesus, He calmed the wind and water with a simple statement.

"Peace, be still."

Together, they had learned over the years to trust in ways that go beyond logic. But this was not a logical night, for it was the night Jesus was betrayed.

— *Chapter 12* —

Living in the Present

WHY SHOULD THE disciples worry at a time like this?

Just a few days before, they had been welcomed into Jerusalem in grand fashion, with a parade and celebration. Jesus had been greeted like a king, with palm branches and shouts of praise.

Perhaps the disciples expected this kind of affirmation, recognition, and appreciation to continue and even expand. After all, that had been a magnificent reception on the streets of Jerusalem.

But on the night He was betrayed, Jesus knew better. On that night, Jesus knew differently. Jesus knew what they did not know. He knew it was all about to change.

Everything was about to change. Never to be the same again.

This would not be a gradual change over a long period of time. It would not be a mere season lasting only two or three months. It would not take months or weeks or even days. It would be a 180-degree turn in a matter of hours. And with each word spoken, prayer prayed, bread eaten, wine sipped, and hymn sung, the minutes ticked by.

Notice again verse 36.

> **LUKE 22:36** *And He said to them, "**But now**, whoever has a money belt is to take it along, likewise also a bag, and whoever has no sword is to sell his coat and buy one."*

Two key words: *But now.*

Jesus had been talking in the past tense, but now Jesus was bringing them back to the present. Back to reality. Back to this night. He would be betrayed with two simple words: "But now."

That was then, but now. That was the way it was back in the day, but now. But now, everything was going to change.

In the past, they didn't need a money belt. *But now,* they would need to take a money belt.

In the past, they didn't need a traveling bag. *But now,* they would need a traveling bag.

In the past, they lacked for nothing. *But now,* whoever had no sword was to sell his coat and buy one.

On the night He was betrayed, Jesus knew that the disciples had to come to grips with the fact that everything would change in a dramatic way. They could no longer rely on the kindness of others, even though they were welcomed just a few days before in grand, ceremonial fashion.

In a matter of hours, all the feet that had just been washed would be walking unchartered paths, with more questions and fears than answers and understanding.

For these disciples, everything they had come to know, embrace, and enjoy was about to change—and never be the same.

Chapter 13

The Sword

I T IS NOT difficult to understand the need to take a money belt and a traveling bag. That part of Jesus's instructions makes sense in a practical way. Not much of a stretch for anyone, regardless of circumstances. There is wisdom in taking care of yourself and being prepared for various situations.

But a sword?

Jesus said, "If you don't have a sword, sell your coat and buy one."

Up to this point, there had not been a hint of violence, other than when Jesus set everyone straight in clearing out the temple. He had raised His voice and turned over tables. And even then, He did not use anything like a sword.

You can almost imagine the complete disbelief on the faces of the disciples as they looked at one another and then at Jesus. They must have thought, "Where is this coming from? Why is Jesus going from washing our feet and talking about sending a Helper and Comforter to now saying we need to buy a sword? Why would He want us to sell our coats and buy swords?"

A coat is worn for warmth and comfort. It is practical. Many people have a favorite coat or sweater. It is something familiar that covers a person in time of need. In a few hours, however, their lives would be anything but comfortable, warm, practical, or familiar.

The life that they had come to know over the past three years was coming to an end. The world that they had come to know over the past three years was coming to an end. A coat would not bring them comfort, warmth, practicality, familiarity, or kindness. A coat would not provide protection in their time of need. A coat would only serve as a false sense of security.

But still, a sword?

The word Jesus used for a sword is the Greek term *machaira*, which means a relatively short sword or another sharp instrument, sword, or dagger. It could also be interpreted as a large knife.[1] So He is not talking about a long sword that a soldier would use but a small sword that could be considered the handgun of the day.[2]

Peter could have thought that Jesus meant he needed to be ready to fight. A sword can help battle against the evil in the world.

---

1. Thayer and Smith. "Greek Lexicon entry for Machaira." https://www.biblestudytools.com/lexicons/greek/kjv/machaira.

2. Dr. Ralph F. Wilson, "98. New Provisions for the Future (Luke 22:35-38)," *Jesus Walk*, http://www.jesuswalk.com/luke/098-provisions.htm.

That is one interpretation, and you could make an argument for it.

James could have thought that Jesus meant he needed to be ready to defend. A sword can help defend from any harm that the world might try to bestow.

That is another interpretation, and you could make an argument for that as well.

James the son of Alpheus, Simon the Zealot, and Judas the son of James all could have thought that Jesus meant they would no longer be in their comfort zones. A sword can indicate a willingness to be uncomfortable facing the world. Perhaps Jesus was preparing them for a world that would become increasingly hostile toward them, to be ready for anything, at any given time, from that moment on.

We don't know exactly what they were thinking. But their minds had to be spinning, trying to figure out what Jesus meant by these mysterious words. Why did He tell them about a sword on this Passover, around this table, in this large, furnished room upstairs?

They were each trying to reconcile the teaching, ministry, and example of Jesus with the idea of selling a coat and buying a sword.

#

Chapter 14

JESUS DID NOT stop to expound on His word. He continued talking to His disciples, referencing the prophet Isaiah. He quoted a portion of a verse from Isaiah 53:12.

> **LUKE 22:37** *"For I tell you that this which is written must be fulfilled in Me, 'And He was numbered with the transgressors'; for that which refers to Me has its fulfillment."*

With this reference, Jesus let His disciples know that the change about to take place would be no accident, surprise, or ambush. The words had been written almost seven hundred years before these thirteen men met for Passover in this large, furnished room upstairs. There had long been anticipation of the fulfillment of these words, but thus far, to no avail. However, on the night Jesus would be betrayed, history would change, and prophecy would be fulfilled.

The context of what Jesus was quoting is aptly known as the chapter of the Suffering Servant.

ISAIAH 53:11-12 *As a result of the anguish of His soul, He will see it and be satisfied; by His knowledge the Righteous One, My Servant, will justify the many, as He will bear their iniquities. Therefore, I will allot Him a portion with the great, and He will divide the booty with the strong; because He poured out Himself to death, and was numbered with the transgressors; yet He Himself bore the sin of many, and interceded for the transgressors.*

The 53rd chapter in Isaiah paints a dark, dreary, graphic, even violent picture of what would happen to Jesus on the night He was betrayed and in the hours that followed.

The disciples were familiar with Isaiah; Jesus had quoted the prophet often. In fact, the first time Jesus preached in a synagogue, He taught from Isaiah. For that, the local people ran Him out of the synagogue and wanted to throw Him off a cliff in Nazareth.

And now, in His last hours with the disciples, He once again quoted from Isaiah.

Part of the chapter of the Suffering Servant says:

ISAIAH 53:3 *He was despised and forsaken of men, a man of sorrows and acquainted with grief; and like one from whom men hide their face He was despised, and we did not esteem Him.*

ISAIAH 53:4 *Surely our griefs He Himself bore, and our sorrows He carried; yet we ourselves esteemed Him stricken, smitten of God, and afflicted.*

ISAIAH 53:5 *But He was pierced through for our transgressions, He was crushed for our iniquities; the chastening for our well-being fell upon Him, and by His scourging we are healed.*

ISAIAH 53:6 *All of us like sheep have gone astray, each of us has turned to his own way; but the Lord has caused the iniquity of us all to fall on Him.*

It was perhaps one of the most personal chapters for Jesus.

Chapter 15

The Fulfillment

THOUGH JESUS QUOTED just a portion of one verse, if the disciples considered the context of that chapter in Isaiah, there would have been a heaviness in the room as the evening progressed.

Jesus fully knew the context of that chapter. He said, "That which is written must be fulfilled *in Me*."

And then Jesus said, "For that which refers *to Me* has its fulfillment."

That one verse is almost hidden among all the others on the night Jesus was betrayed, yet it is vital to understand what would happen in just a few hours.

Fulfillment.

A two-fold fulfillment: "fulfilled *in* Me" and "refers *to* Me has its fulfillment."

The words of the prophets written hundreds of years before that night would find their long-awaited fulfillment in Christ Jesus, the Messiah. Through the inspiration of the Spirit of God, Isaiah had insight into that which would take place six centuries after He penned the words on parchment.

Everything that would take place within the next twenty-four hours would happen as a fulfillment. Not a surprise. Not a military ambush. Not a religious conspiracy. It all had to happen.

There was no other option.

That which had been prophesied would be fulfilled *in* Christ and *to* Christ. There was going to be a cost.

Jesus did not want these disciples gathered in the large, furnished room upstairs to miss that bit of truth. Part of the fulfillment was that Jesus would be "numbered with transgressors." The word "numbered" does not mean He would be hanging between two thieves, though He did. That interpretation would be too limiting for the fulfillment.

The word "numbered" is the Greek word *logizamai*, which means "to reckon, count, compute, calculate." The word deals with reality and facts, not suppositions. If I *logizomai* that my bank account has twenty-five dollars in it, then the account has twenty-five dollars in it as a matter of fact. Otherwise, I would be deceiving myself and others.[3]

These prophetic words show that Jesus would be counted, numbered, and credited with transgressors. There would be a cost incurred. The sins of the world would be upon Him as He would be crucified on a cross in just a few hours. And

---

3. Thayer and Smith. "Greek Lexicon entry for Logizomai." www.biblestudytools.com/lexicon, 1999.

this was going to happen so "that which is written" would be fulfilled by Jesus.

Peter understood this truth years later as He reflected on this night that Jesus was betrayed and the hours that followed. He even referenced part of Isaiah 53:5 in his writing.

> **1 PETER 2:24-25** *And He Himself bore our sins in His body on the cross, so that we might die to sin and live to righteousness; for **by His wounds you were healed**. For you were continually straying like sheep, but now you have returned to the Shepherd and Guardian of your souls.*

As John MacArthur has said, "So the worst that men can do turns out to be the fulfillment of God's plan."[4] Jesus gave this brief but incredibly significant word to show that Isaiah 53 was being fulfilled, moment by moment, on the night He was betrayed.

It was a somber and reflective moment. A vulnerable and emotional moment.

Jesus was treated as a sinner on our behalf.

And it was God's plan.

Do not miss the significance of the truth and fulfillment of Isaiah 53. In that chapter by the prophet Isaiah, there are twenty different instances showing that the Suffering Servant would be treated as a sinner. Jesus was fulfilling Isaiah's words completely on the night He was betrayed.

---

4. John MacArthur, "Table Talk on Trouble and Triumph, Part 3," *Grace to You*, March 2, 2008, https://www.gty.org/library/sermons-library/42-272/table-talk-on-trouble-and-triumph-part-3.

Some would say it cost nothing, but there is always a cost. The price had to be paid. According to Isaiah 53—and what Jesus had just told His disciples—it would be a severe cost.

It would be unlike anything that had ever happened before or since.

Chapter 16

The Response

THE DISCIPLES STILL did not comprehend the significance of the price to be paid.

Jesus had just shared with them a glimpse of heavenly revelation, something that Isaiah had written and prophesied almost seven hundred years ago. The words were coming into fulfillment within the next few hours. But the disciples' response showed their lack of understanding.

> **LUKE 22:38** *They said, "Lord, look, here are two swords." And He said to them, "It is enough."*

You can almost picture Jesus dropping His head, rubbing His temples, shaking His head in disbelief. Perhaps thinking to Himself, "Really? This is how you respond?"

There was cause for worry. The disciples still didn't get it, and time was moving quickly. More than three years of lessons, training, traveling, and ministering were all coming down to this moment. This time, this hour. This response.

Jesus did not want to go into any further discussion. With almost a sigh of exasperation, He said, "It is enough." And that concluded the dialogue. Jesus knew they would learn the meaning of the lesson soon enough.

Luke recorded Jesus's next move. The Gospel of Luke says He went to the garden.

LUKE 22:39 *And He came out and proceeded as was His custom to the Mount of Olives; and the disciples also followed Him.*

John gives us greater detail of the teaching of Jesus in that large, furnished room upstairs that the other Gospels do not. But Luke details the next step: out the door, to the garden. Each of the Gospels lets us know that Jesus and the disciples left the large, furnished room upstairs. Matthew and Mark say that "after singing hymns," they went out to the Mount of Olives. John merely says they "got up and left."

But notice Luke once again lets us know something unique. He says that Jesus proceeded, "as was His custom," to the Mount of Olives. On the night Jesus was betrayed, He went to a very familiar place. It was a place He and the disciples had been before, perhaps many times over the years. But sometimes places of familiarity are where we are the most vulnerable, even in a garden.

Jesus and the eleven remaining disciples—Judas would have already left the room—made their way to the garden. It was a familiar pathway. By this time, it was late into the night, possibly approaching midnight. On their walk, they would have crossed a ravine with a little brook running through it called the Kidron Valley. To the east of the Kidron Valley lay the Mount of Olives and the Garden of Gethsemane.

The group would have walked out of Jerusalem, down the steep slope into the Kidron Valley, up the side of the Mount of Olives, and then into the familiar Garden of Gethsemane.

Chapter 17

The Garden

THIS GARDEN FELT like home for Jesus. It was familiar. It was peaceful and quiet. It was a place of refuge.

Except this was the night He was betrayed.

Nevertheless, the beauty of the garden was such that Jesus taught lessons based on His surroundings. On the night He was betrayed, Jesus taught the disciples lessons about the vine and the branches. He used the garden as an object lesson about their relationship. Jesus was the vine, and they were the branches. Apart from Jesus they could do nothing.

In the days, weeks, months, and years ahead, the disciples would come to realize the significance of this lesson from the garden. It was a truth that would empower them in ways they could not imagine on the night they walked this garden path.

It was on the night He was betrayed that Jesus did what He would often do in difficult situations, especially when He was in the garden. He prayed.

He prayed with an intensity that He never had before. He prayed to the point where His sweat was like drops of blood (Luke 22:44). The heart of Jesus was aching and grieving. His heart was torn knowing what His purpose was from the beginning—not the beginning in Bethlehem, but the beginning of all beginnings, from the beginning of creation.

It was in the garden where He laid His heart before His Abba Father, His daddy. His Father, with whom He had created this garden before there was man or beast. And now, in this garden on the night He was betrayed, Jesus prayed. And prayed. And prayed. And prayed.

He prayed for His disciples, who were gathered not far from where He was. He prayed for the world and for the disciples to come.

JOHN 17:20 *"I do not ask on behalf of these alone, but for those also who believe in Me through their word."*

Jesus also prayed for His cup to pass, knowing the physical pain and humiliation that was about to transpire. But ultimately, He prayed for the will of God, Abba Father, to be fulfilled.

Jesus had asked the disciples to keep watch, knowing what was about to take place as the hour drew near. But the disciples fell asleep in the garden, the place of familiarity. They fell asleep not once, not twice, but three times, each time succumbing to their weaknesses and selfishness (Matthew 26:36-46).

None of them understood the magnitude of what was taking place in that moment of time.

Chapter 18

The Time Had Come

WHILE JESUS PRAYED and the disciples nodded off, a crowd of people formed outside the garden. Soldiers, mockers, religious leaders, and the betrayer gathered. The time had come.

> **LUKE 22:47** *While He was still speaking, behold, a crowd came, and the one called Judas, one of the twelve, was preceding them; and he approached Jesus to kiss Him.*

Jesus had finished praying. He was not sitting and waiting. He was not hiding or running away. Jesus was teaching.

As He was speaking, a crowd came. The garden had been occupied by the eleven remaining disciples and Jesus in the darkness of the night. By this time, it was the dark, early morning hours. The quietness of the garden had been quiet enough for prayer and for unplanned sleep. Now, a crowd was coming. The quietness had ceased, and the noise of soldiers and mockers had taken over, including the footsteps of one named Judas.

Up to this moment, no one knew where Judas had gone when he left that large, furnished room upstairs. No one had tried to stop him. They had guessed he was leaving to take care of treasury business of some sort.

But now, they all knew.

The remaining eleven disciples saw Judas, who had traveled with them throughout the regions of Galilee, Judea, Samaria, and Jerusalem. Judas, who had been with them on the side of the mountain listening to the first sermon Jesus taught. Judas, who had his feet washed a few hours before, along with the other eleven. Those washed feet were facing Jesus. Feet to feet, face to face, eye to eye. And now those washed feet were standing in front of a crowd.

Judas didn't come alone. That would have been the brave thing to do. That would have been the confident thing to do. But Judas was neither brave nor confident. He came with a crowd.

Some translations use the word "mob"; John uses the phrase *Roman cohort*, a term for part of a legion. No one knew exactly how many were there. It could have been anywhere from thirty to six hundred people. It did not matter how many there were.

It was only a few hours earlier in that large, furnished room upstairs that Jesus had told His disciples that Scripture must be fulfilled *in Him* and *to Him*. This was no surprise. This was no accident or ambush. The hour had come, and there is always a cost. The price had to be paid. The betrayer had arrived.

LUKE 22:48-50 *But Jesus said to him, "Judas, are you betraying the Son of Man with a kiss?" When those who were around Him saw what was going to happen, they said, "Lord, shall we strike with the sword?" And one of them struck the slave of the high priest and cut off his right ear.*

The kiss was a greeting for a friend or family member. It was never intended for the one you betrayed. The gentleness of the kiss gave way to the graveness of the situation.

When those around Jesus—namely the eleven remaining disciples—understood what was about to happen, they had an aha moment. They remembered what Jesus had said around the table in the large, furnished room upstairs.

This must have been why they needed swords.

Chapter 19

The Sword and a Miracle

WHEN JUDAS REVEALED himself as a betrayer, the disciples' minds must have spun. "This is what Jesus was talking about," they thought. "This is why we needed a sword."

One of the disciples—John tells us it was Peter—grabbed the sword and cut off the right ear of the servant of the high priest. John tells us his name was Malchus.

On the night He was betrayed, the disciples still did not understand fully. They didn't get it. A sword to cut off the ear of Malchus?

If Jesus had wanted, He could have simply whispered under His breath, "Now." The heavens would have opened, the stars could very well have moved to the side, and a legion of angels could be swooping down in all directions—swooping down and annihilating the crowd, the mob, and the soldiers.

If Jesus had wanted, He could have said, "Let the winds blow." The vines that Jesus had talked about with the disciples would have started swaying. The tree branches would have started moving, and the leaves would have started falling. The wind would have started whirling in such a magnitude that a tornado could have lifted each person in the crowd off the ground into the air. Each soldier who had come, and even the betrayer named Judas, would have been lifted off their feet, completely incapacitated. The wind of a tornado could have ended the entire ordeal.

But a sword? That was never what Jesus intended.

It is in that moment that Luke lets us in on something the other Gospel writers do not.

LUKE 22:51 *But Jesus answered and said, "Stop! No more of this." And He touched his ear and healed him.*

We often think of the raising of Lazarus as the last miracle Jesus performed before His final journey to the cross. It was indeed a foreshadowing of what was to come in a matter of days with Jesus. The raising of Lazarus from the tomb was dramatic, to say the least, eye-opening for the witnesses who had gathered around and the last straw for those wanting to silence Jesus. But it was not the last public miracle.

In the darkness of the early morning hours in the Garden of Gethsemane, a very subtle miracle took place. Before a crowd of people that included soldiers of the Roman Empire, religious leaders, disciples, and a betrayer, Jesus healed the ear of Malchus.

Some might not have noticed. Others might not have cared. Malchus was not a follower of Jesus; he was simply doing his job in the moment, perhaps not even caring who Jesus was or what He stood for. He hadn't even asked to be healed. The word used for "ear" means it could have been a mere portion of his ear that had been cut off, such as the ear lobe, which arguably makes the incident even more insignificant.

But there was nothing insignificant about this miracle. On the night He was betrayed, in the very moment Jesus was betrayed, He showed compassion.

Jesus showed compassion on the one who was there to arrest Him, the one who was there to take Him down and silence Him. In front of the mob of people, the religious leaders, the soldiers, the military leaders, and the disciples, Jesus did something that was not dramatic or larger than life. He did not heal for the fanfare or because of the gathered crowd. He did it for the individual named Malchus.

It was not unlike just a few hours earlier when Jesus had washed the feet of all His disciples, including the one who would betray Him. No fanfare, no crowd. Just a servant leader showing compassion for each individual, one by one.

The healing of Malchus's ear was not as fascinating as raising Lazarus from the dead. It was not as dramatic as healing the woman who had been hemorrhaging for years—the woman who had simply reached out and touched the robe of Jesus. It was not as enjoyable as turning water into wine.

It was simply healing the ear of a man named Malchus. John continues with the story in John 18.

JOHN 18:12 *So the Roman cohort and the commander and the officers of the Jews arrested Jesus and bound Him, and led Him to Annas first; for he was father-in-law of Caiaphas, who was high priest that year.*

The sword was put back into the sheath. It was not the time. It was not the place. It was not the purpose.

It was time to drink the cup given by the Father.

It was time to be arrested and bound. It was time for the betrayal to be completed.

This was not just business as usual. It was not a bargain to be negotiated. It was not without cost. There is always a cost. On the night He was betrayed, Jesus paid the price in the garden.

For the eleven remaining disciples, and for us, life would never be the same.

Chapter 20

The Lesson

HOW OFTEN DO we miss the little miracles of Jesus? We look for the fascinating. We hope for the dramatic. We wait for the enjoyable.

But the miracles of Jesus do not always happen the way we imagine or expect. They do not always take place in a worship service inside a church building. The miracles of Jesus do not always take place in secluded retreats during moments of silence.

We look for the extraordinary, and we miss the ordinary.

We miss the simple touch of Jesus. We miss His touch to our ear, which allows us to hear Him when He speaks.

Are we listening, watching, and learning? The Scripture at our fingertips reveals the truth of eternity past, present, and future. The words of Isaiah foretold what would happen in a stable behind an overcrowded inn in Bethlehem. Even the kiss of betrayal is a reminder of how easy it is to turn away from what we once believed.

On the night He was betrayed, Jesus wanted His disciples to understand the significance of each detail. What began as an annual Passover tradition in a large, furnished room upstairs turned into a kiss of betrayal and an arrest. History was changed for a mere thirty pieces of silver.

The cost would never be calculated with the limitations of the monetary. The cost would be more severe than silver. The cost would be blood shed of the innocent in place of the guilty.

There is always a cost, even on the darkest of nights.

3

The Darkness

Introduction

From the beginning of creation, there was darkness.

GENESIS 1:1-2 *In the beginning God created the heavens and the earth. The earth was formless and void, and darkness was over the surface of the deep, and the Spirit of God was moving over the surface of the waters.*

On a very basic level, darkness can be scary and intimidating. It can be overwhelming and overpowering at times. Darkness was in the beginning. Before light was created, there was darkness. Over the surface of the deep, there was darkness. In the vastness of time and space, there was darkness.

But remember: in the beginning, as the darkness was over the surface of the deep, Scripture says, "And the Spirit of God was moving over the surface of the waters." The Spirit of God was never intimidated, overwhelmed, or overpowered by darkness.

It was in that moment—the moment of the Spirit of God in darkness—when everything changed. It was then that God said, "Let there be light" (Genesis 1:3). And there was light.

In the beginning of creation, in the midst of the darkness with the Spirit of God moving over the surface of the waters, a candle was lit for all eternity.

God saw that the light was good. God separated the light from the darkness, calling the light day and the darkness night (Genesis 1:3-5). Light shines in the darkness, but the darkness did not and could not comprehend the light (John 1:5). Darkness did not understand the candle that had been lit at the beginning of creation. Darkness did not realize that everything shifted when light was spoken into existence. The darkness became a mere shadow.

Darkness is not powerful. It is not overwhelming. Darkness is not intimidating. It is not scary.

However, darkness is real. Darkness is very real. It is necessary to be contrasted with the light and the candle to be lit. The light was designed and created to shine in the darkness, in the shadows, in the bleakest of times, in the dreary gloom of the moment.

The light was designed to shine in the darkest of nights, even on the night Jesus was betrayed.

— Chapter 21 —

Do You Understand?

THE NIGHT JESUS was betrayed began with a meal in a large, furnished room upstairs. The twelve disciples gathered around the table to celebrate the Passover, which had been commemorated by the Jewish people since the days of Moses.

As the meal was in progress, a conversation turned into a dispute about who would be greatest among them. Jesus, the leader of the group, got up from the table during the meal and showed them what greatness really looks like. He knelt before them one by one and washed their feet. The feet of each disciple were washed by the hands of their leader, Jesus. He didn't leave anyone out, including Judas Iscariot.

After washing their feet, Jesus returned to the table and asked the disciples if they understood what He had done for them. It was a simple question. He had asked the disciples many questions over their years of traveling and ministry together. This was simply a follow-up question to what He had just done for them.

The question did not seem to be rhetorical. It seemed Jesus expected them to answer quickly. But that did not happen. Instead, there was silence. No response. No guess.

Just silence.

So Jesus answered His own question. He explained that He had given them an example of what they should do for one another.

> **JOHN 13:13-15** *You call Me Teacher and Lord; and you are right, for so I am. If I then, the Lord and the Teacher, washed your feet, you also ought to wash one another's feet. For I gave you an example that you also should do as I did to you.*

If Jesus had stopped there, it would have been a sweet lesson for the disciples to learn. A lesson with a visual and an application expressed with great clarity. Jesus was their Teacher, and they had recognized Him as such for three years. Three years of miles traveled and lessons taught. Jesus was the Lord, the Messiah who had been foretold by the prophets. Peter had made a bold and confident proclamation of that fact in Caesarea Philippi.

> **MATTHEW 16:16** *Simon Peter answered, "You are the Messiah, the Son of the living God." (NIV)*

The disciples knew these facts about Jesus to be real and even personal. Jesus knew they knew. Jesus knew they recognized these things. It would have been a sweet, intimate, personal moment if Jesus had only stopped speaking.

But He did not stop with those words. Jesus continued speaking words that would capture their attention like never before.

Chapter 22

Truly I Say to You

THE DISCIPLES' FEET had just been washed by the One they had been following for more than three years. The One whose feet had walked on water, the One who gave sight to the blind and caused the lame to walk. Their feet had just been washed by the One who touched the untouchables of the day, the lepers. The One who was light in the darkness, the Light of the world.

Their Teacher and Lord was not finished speaking. Back at the table, Jesus said words that would shake the disciples to their core. His words were recorded by Mark:

> **MARK 14:18-19** *And as they were reclining at table and eating, Jesus said, "Truly, I say to you, one of you will betray me, one who is eating with me." They began to be sorrowful and to say to him one after another, "Is it I?" (ESV)*

It was supposed to be the traditional, annual Passover meal, a celebration to reflect and remember that which God had done for His people in the days of Moses. A celebration of deliverance from the darkness of bondage, slavery, and captivity. A celebration of freedom in the darkness of night in the days of Moses. It was supposed to be a festive occasion.

Then it turned into a dispute.

And then it turned into a foot washing.

And then it turned into a life lesson.

And then? Then it turned into a betrayal.

No one saw it coming. Well, eleven in the room did not see it coming.

Imagine the setting in that large, furnished room upstairs. Gathered back at the table, continuing the meal that had been interrupted by the foot washing and brief life lesson, Jesus said, "Truly I say to you, one of you will betray Me, one who is eating with Me" (Mark 14:18).

The disciples' ears must have perked up when they heard that first word, "truly." In Greek, it is "amen." The significance of the word is based on its location in the sentence. For instance, when "amen" is used at the beginning of the sentence, it means, "What I'm about to say is the truth, with certainty." When the word is used at the end of a sentence, it means, "So be it; may it be fulfilled."

Jesus began the sentence with "amen." What He was about to say was the truth, with certainty.

Truly. Perhaps Matthew was bringing a piece of bread to his mouth when He heard the word and stopped in mid-air.

Truly. Perhaps Peter took a deep breath, waiting with anticipation for what followed.

With one word, Jesus had their attention. The mood had transitioned again.

"Truly I say to you that one of you will betray Me—one who is eating with Me."

At that moment, if any of the disciples still had a loaf of bread or a cup of wine in their hands, they would have put it down cautiously, in silence.

"Truly I say to you."

It sank in.

The disciples may not have always been quick to understand Jesus over the years. They were a work in progress.

But this they understood.

They realized, one by one, that *all* of them were eating with Jesus. All twelve disciples were seated at this table in the large, furnished room upstairs in the darkness of the night, which seemed to be growing darker by the moment.

It became obvious to the twelve disciples: this was no ordinary Passover meal. This was different from anything they had ever experienced in their lifetime, not to mention over the past three years together.

This large, furnished room upstairs was feeling increasingly small. There was nowhere to hide in this room lit by candles while the Light of the World captured their attention.

"Truly I say to you."

Chapter 23

Stunned

EARLIER IN THE evening, there had been a dispute about who among them would be greatest. All twelve of them had their feet washed by Jesus, and after seeing an example of the greatest becoming the servant to all, they no longer disputed who would be greatest.

Their Servant Leader, their Teacher, the Lord Jesus Himself, said one of them would betray Him. One whose feet had been washed. One who had accepted the call to follow Him. One who saw the Son of God walking on the water. One of the twelve sitting around the table in the large, furnished room upstairs on the darkest of nights would do the unthinkable. One of them would betray Jesus.

All twelve disciples were around the table for one another to see.

For Jesus to see.

Eyes moved to look at one another. Eyes avoided looking directly at the Light of the World.

As they listened to Jesus speak heart-wrenching, life-changing, mood-shifting words, something interesting took place. Or, more appropriately, it is interesting to notice what did *not* take place.

John tells us in his Gospel they were stunned.

JOHN 13:22 *The disciples began looking at one another, at a loss to know of which one He was speaking.*

There was an uneasiness around the table as they each looked at one another, at a loss for words. Yet no one pointed a finger.

It could have been brother against brother. Andrew could have turned on Peter, pointing a finger of accusation. James could have turned on John, pointing a finger of accusation.

It could have been Judas against Judas: Judas Iscariot pointing a finger towards Judas the son of James. It could have been the lesser-known disciples turning on one another: James the son of Alpheus, turning to Simon the Zealot, pointing a finger of blame because this sounded like something a Zealot would do.

But none of that happened. They did not turn against each other. There was no finger-pointing. No blame. No dissension. Instead, each disciple turned inward.

They each knew.

After three years of listening to Jesus teach . . . after three years of watching Jesus heal and serve . . . three years of learning life lessons, sometimes taught from a boat or hillside, other times from a synagogue, or, such as this night, in a large, furnished room upstairs . . .

They each knew that when darkness came, their courage caved. The fingers of blame were pointed inward.

In the darkness of that night, in the darkness of the moment, the darkness of the words hung in the air. The words hung in the air of that large, furnished room upstairs.

They each knew.

Nathaniel knew. Matthew knew.

James and his brother John knew. Peter and his brother Andrew knew.

Phillip knew. James the son of Alpheus knew. Simon the Zealot knew. Thomas had no doubt; he knew. Judas, the son of James, knew.

And the other Judas—Judas Iscariot—knew what no one else knew.

They each knew it could be them.

Chapter 24

Is it I?

THE MOOD HAD shifted. The disciples were no longer celebrating the Passover but grieving Jesus's words. Mark recorded it like this:

> **MARK 14:19** *They began to be sorrowful and to say to him one after another, "Is it I?" (ESV)*

This would not be the last time Peter would feel sorrow and grieve like this. The Greek word *lupeo* is the same word used in John's Gospel to describe how Peter felt when Jesus asked him for a third time, "Do you love me?" *Lupeo* goes beyond mere sorrow to a deeper pain from within.

Nathaniel grieved, as did Matthew. John grieved. As Jesus's words about betrayal began to sink in, each of the twelve began to grieve. Their hearts not only sank but ached. In the darkness of the night, in the darkness of the moment, in the darkness of despair, each of the disciples grieved.

And, one by one, they began to speak.

Phillip began to speak. He was still in disbelief of what he had just heard. Not wanting to look up or make eye contact with the One who had just washed his feet, Phillip perhaps kept his head lowered and said, not much above a whisper, "Is it I?"

Andrew began to speak. Perhaps he remembered the time he had questioned whether Jesus could feed five thousand men plus women and children with a mere five barley loaves and two fish. Andrew may have closed his eyes and remembered the words that had come out of his mouth: "What are these for so many people?" (John 6:9). Andrew had not believed it could be possible. This time, Andrew asked Jesus another question of which he was not proud and of which he knew was possible: "Is it I?"

As Matthew began to speak, he may have remembered all that he had given up. He had given up fortune and would never have fame as a tax collector. Matthew had given up all that he had known: his livelihood, his connection to Rome, the table at which he had been sitting when Jesus first approached him. With all that he had sacrificed, Matthew knew what he did not want to acknowledge. A question needed to be asked. With a reserved voice in the direction of where Jesus was seated, Matthew asked, "Is it I?"

Perhaps Nathaniel thought about the time Jesus saw him sitting under a fig tree, even when Jesus was not anywhere to be seen. He remembered being known by Jesus without ever meeting Him before. Nathaniel was, in the words of Jesus, "a true Israelite in whom there is no deceit." Now, wishing he were back in simpler times under that fig tree, Nathaniel spoke words that sounded like deceit. "Is it I?"

James may have regretted the times he had asked for something more. More recognition. More visibility in glory, sitting on the right side. James may have realized in the darkness of this moment that "more" meant nothing. Keeping his head bowed, lifting only his eyes, he asked with fearful resolve, "Is it I?"

Hearing the question from the lips of his brother James, perhaps John realized that even those closest to and most beloved by Jesus were vulnerable. No one was exempt from being in the darkness. After his brother asked, so did John. "Is it I?"

Thomas was probably afraid to ask the question he had just heard six times. He had never been afraid to ask Jesus a question about anything, even for clarification purposes. But now he had to ask what his heart already knew: it was possible it was him. He had to say it out loud, not for Jesus to hear and not for the others to hear, but for himself to hear. With a deep breath, he asked, "Is it I?"

James the son of Alpheus realized there was nowhere to hide. Nowhere to turn. No longer possible to be anonymous. With resignation and sadness, he said, "Is it I?"

Simon the Zealot may have shriveled inside at the darkness of Jesus's words. He had been trained to take over and push through during difficulties and challenges, to never give up or give in. He had been trained to be confident in all circumstances. But now, with a crackling voice and no hint of confidence, he asked, "Is it I?"

Judas the son of James watched his friends around the table speak, one by one. Having listened to the question that none of them wanted to ask but were each compelled to ask, he knew he was not stronger than the others. He was not bolder. He was just like all of them, a follower of the One who had washed his feet. And with that stark reality, he said, "Is it I?"

Peter probably took a deep breath and held it, exhaling slowly before taking another deep breath. Hold. Exhale. Deep breath. Hold. Exhale. Deep breath. He breathed deeply as he listened to these men with whom he had served, traveled, and fished all ask the same unimaginable question. He may have noticed it grow more difficult to breathe as he heard the voices of Nathaniel and Phillip and James and John. Even his own brother Andrew had asked the unimaginable question. Peter, the rock, must have felt like a grain of sand knowing he had to ask what he knew was true. Peter said what he never thought would come out of his mouth. In the darkness of the moment, Peter asked Jesus, the Son of the Living God, "Is it I?"

Then there was Judas Iscariot. Having heard each of the eleven ask the question, he probably sat in stunned silence, never thinking it would unfold like this. Judas knew these men by name and reputation, yet he sat and let each one of them ask the question. It was a night of betrayal as the words echoed in the room, "Is it I?"

Judas was no longer able to ignore the face of Jesus. No longer able to ignore the eyes of Jesus. No longer able to ignore the words of Jesus. In the darkness of the moment, perhaps with a hint of guilt and even shame, he may have locked eyes with Jesus. It probably felt as if the other eleven had disappeared. Judas had to say what needed to be said. "Is it I?"

The darkness was over the surface of the deep. The darkness was real. The darkness was necessary. In that moment around the table, in the large, furnished room upstairs, the darkness became darker on the night that Jesus was betrayed.

Chapter 25

You Will All Fall Away

E ACH OF THE disciples had asked the question, "Is it I?" They each knew it was possible, and it had grieved them.

Now Jesus had more to say. He quoted the prophet Zechariah.

MATTHEW 26:31-33 *Then Jesus said to them, "You will all fall away because of Me this night, for it is written: 'I will strike the shepherd, and the sheep of the flock will be scattered.' But after I have been raised, I will go ahead of you to Galilee." But Peter replied to Him, "Even if they all fall away because of You, I will never fall away!"*

Jesus predicted, "You will all fall away because of Me this night."

It had begun as "one out of twelve" who would betray him. But now Jesus said "all" would fall away.

Each of the disciples had asked three words: "Is it I?" But now, in the haunting silence from within themselves were the same three words, though this time without an inflection. "It is I."

The darkest of nights continued growing darker by the moment. But did you notice the candle in the night? Did you notice the glimmer of light in the darkness?

The darkness was over the surface of the deep, and the Spirit of God was moving. There was a flicker of light. Without any explanation or elaboration, Jesus says matter of factly, "But after I have been raised."

The disciples were so overcome by the darkness of the moment that they missed the glimmer of light, the flicker of the candle. There was a spark, and with a blink of an eye, they missed it.

Peter was not focused on the candle. He ignored the glimmer of the light. He looked beyond the spark and thought about himself. Peter said, "Even if they all fall away because of You, I will never fall away!" With these words, Peter elevated himself above the other disciples.

Peter believed his own words because he was the one who had stood up boldly in Caesarea Philippi and declared to Jesus, "You are the Christ, the Son of the Living God." He was known as a rock, immovable, steady, and faithful at all costs. Peter was the one who had willingly stepped out of the boat and onto the water to walk toward Jesus. Peter had been willing to do whatever it took to follow Jesus.

Not only that, but Jesus seemed to have confirmed it in Caesarea Philippi. He had said to Peter, "Blessed are you, Simon Barjona, because flesh and blood did not reveal this to you, but My Father who is in heaven. And I also say to you that you are Peter, and upon this rock I will build My church; and the gates of Hades will not overpower it" (Matthew 16:17-18). In Peter's mind, he had many reasons to believe he would never fall away from Jesus on a dark night like this.

But in that large, furnished room upstairs, Peter's moment of confidence was interrupted by a response from Jesus. The response was much different than what Peter had heard at Caesarea Philippi.

MATTHEW 26:34 *Jesus said to him, "Truly I say to you that this very night, before a rooster crows, you will deny Me three times."*

Truly. Peter must have cringed when he heard that first word in the original Greek language. Amen. Peter knew that what Jesus said was the truth, with certainty.

And the darkness was over the surface of the deep in the large, furnished room upstairs.

— Chapter 26 —

Not Me

PETER PUSHED BACK, perhaps trying to stand with the same strength and boldness as he had done previous times in previous conversations. But on this occasion, his legs were weakening by the moment, a nervous rhythmic movement of which he was unaware but which Jesus noticed. Nevertheless, Peter made a proclamation.

> **MATTHEW 26:35** *Peter said to Him, "Even if I have to die with You, I will not deny You!" All the disciples said the same thing as well.*

Peter would rather die with Jesus than deny knowing Him. As the other disciples listened to Peter, they felt they could do the same. But between their recent affirmations of Peter's statement and the previous "Is it I?" responses to Jesus's words, they knew which was more real. Truly, they each knew.

The night was growing darker as they walked to the garden according to the Gospel of Matthew. In the garden, there were lessons and prayers. And for the disciples, there was sleep—even though there was not supposed to be any sleep on the darkest of nights. Not while the darkness was over the deep, in the depths of the garden on the night He was betrayed. Yet the disciples fell asleep. The spirit was willing, but their flesh was weak.

Jesus woke them from their sleep three times. The third time would be the final wake-up call before the betrayal.

MATTHEW 26:45-46 *Then He came to the disciples and said to them, "Are you still sleeping and resting? Behold, the hour is at hand and the Son of Man is being betrayed into the hands of sinners. Get up, let's go; behold, the one who is betraying Me is near!"*

After having dozed off the third time, perhaps their first thought when they heard the words of Jesus was, "Is it I?" They were supposed to stay awake, and they kept falling asleep. "Is it I?" The night grew darker by the moment.

Then Judas returned. They didn't know where he had gone when he left the large, furnished room upstairs. But now he had returned. And he was not alone. It seemed to catch everyone off guard except Jesus.

The eyes of the disciples must have locked on Judas, watching in disbelief. Judas walked straight toward Jesus with an army of Roman soldiers following him. Then came the kiss of betrayal.

The deed was complete. The soldiers instantly surrounded Jesus, and Peter stepped in with a sword to cut off the ear of one of the servants named Malchus. Peter was willing to die for Jesus, putting his own life on the line in this dark moment in the garden.

But Jesus told Peter to stop. He told all who were gathered on the night He was betrayed to stop, for those who take up the sword will die by the sword (Matthew 26:52).

All He had to do was call on His Father, and at once there would be twelve legions of angels at His disposal (Matthew 26:53).

— *Chapter 27* —

Time to Run

JESUS DID NOT call on His Father. Nor did twelve legions of angels appear. Instead, Jesus said something more.

MATTHEW 26:55-56 *At that time Jesus said to the crowds, "Have you come out with swords and clubs to arrest Me as you would against a man inciting a revolt? Every day I used to sit within the temple grounds teaching, and you did not arrest Me. But all this has taken place so that the Scriptures of the prophets will be fulfilled." Then all the disciples left Him and fled.*

All of these events took place so that the Scripture of the prophets would be fulfilled, including the impossible: all the disciples left Jesus and fled. In His greatest time of need, the disciples fled the One they had followed for more than three years.

The feet of Phillip that had been washed by Jesus a few hours earlier now ran away from Jesus. The feet of Andrew and James and Thomas ran, fleeing the One who had washed their feet.

Each of the eleven disciples fled on the feet that had been washed, deserting Jesus on the night He was betrayed.

As they ran past vines and branches, perhaps they were haunted by the words, "Is it I?" As they ran past the Mount of Olives, perhaps they could not get out of their minds, "Is it I?"

Those washed feet now ran down the slope of the garden, across the brook of the ravine of the Kidron Valley, each stride pounding out a question: "Is it I?"

They ran through the streets of Jerusalem and around corners. "Is it I?"

Their breath grew shorter and heavier with each step. "Is it I?"

They discovered the darkness after each turn. "Is it I?"

Then they rounded a corner and stopped abruptly.

Perhaps Nathaniel saw it first. Philip and Andrew might have seen it next. Maybe James and John were close behind. The others might have gone in a different direction—every man for himself.

Each desperately tried to catch his breath. In the dark silence of the night, they probably didn't look at each other. They probably didn't speak. But one by one, they may have looked up.

The window.

The window of the large, furnished room upstairs. The window where the evening began with a simple, annual Passover meal.

As they stopped and stared upward, still breathing heavily, they did not know what to do next. In the quietness of the moment, in the darkness of the night, they whispered to themselves so no one would hear.

"It is I."

Chapter 28

Another Kind of Betrayal

WHILE THE DISCIPLES ran, Jesus was arrested and taken to the High Priest. Judas, the betrayer, carried out his deed while Peter appeared to be keeping his word. Peter had not completely fled like the other disciples but watched from a distance.

> **MATTHEW 26:58** *But Peter was following Him at a distance, as far as the courtyard of the high priest, and he came inside and sat down with the officers to see the outcome.*

They kindled a fire and sat in the courtyard—a glimmer of light in the darkness. Peter was close enough to watch the injustice. Perhaps he was not as bold as before, but at least he followed Jesus, even if at a distance. He was in a position to make a stand when needed and if appropriate.

MATTHEW 26:69 *Now Peter was sitting outside in the courtyard, and a slave woman came to him and said, "You too were with Jesus the Galilean."*

This was Peter's opportunity. For a split second, he may have wanted to stand up and repeat the proclamation he made in Caesarea Philippi: "Jesus of Galilee is the Christ, the Son of the Living God." But the darkness was over the deep of this courtyard, and the echo of words came back to his mind: "Is it I?"

MATTHEW 26:70 *But he denied it before them all, saying, "I do not know what you are talking about."*

The light of the campfire could not overtake the darkness of the moment. The courtyard seemed to be getting smaller. Peter needed to step away in shame and reflection. "Is it I?"

MATTHEW 26:71 *When he had gone out to the gateway, another slave woman saw him and said to those who were there, "This man was with Jesus of Nazareth."*

Peter wanted desperately to become invisible. If he had only run away with the other disciples, he would not be in this position. If he closed his eyes, he would have heard the voice in his head, "Is it I?"

MATTHEW 26:72 *And again he denied it, with an oath: "I do not know the man."*

With one denial came shame. And remorse. He had failed once again. There was nowhere to hide, nowhere to turn.

MATTHEW 26:73 *A little later the bystanders came up and said to Peter, "You really are one of them as well, since even the way you talk gives you away."*

Peter wished he could have kept his mouth shut. But they heard his voice and accent, and they could tell that Peter was associated with Jesus.

MATTHEW 26:74 *Then he began to curse and swear, "I do not know the man!" And immediately a rooster crowed.*

The rooster. Peter wondered if anyone else had heard it. He had heard roosters before, but this rooster was different. This rooster made a sound that Peter would never forget. The convicting crow echoed across the darkness of the night.

The harsh reality set in.

MATTHEW 26:75 *And Peter remembered the statement that Jesus had made: "Before a rooster crows, you will deny Me three times." And he went out and wept bitterly.*

"Is it I?" The question became a statement. "It is I." Like the other disciples, Peter realized there are all kinds of betrayal beyond a kiss on the cheek.

Chapter 29

The Lesson

IT WAS A long night. It was a dark night. It was a sad night. There was betrayal and running. There was denying and weeping.

And it had all started with a meal. It had started with conversations, lessons, and washing of feet. It had started out in remembrance and celebration of God's deliverance of His people in the days of Moses.

It was a night of purpose for another kind of deliverance.

On the night Jesus was betrayed, the darkness was over the deep in a large, furnished room upstairs. The darkness was in the garden where Jesus prayed. The darkness was in the streets of Jerusalem where disciples ran.

But the darkness does not overwhelm or intimidate God. It is necessary to be contrasted with the light and the candle to be lit.

It was in the midst of the darkness, the darkest of the dark, that the Spirit of God moved. The Spirit moved in the large, furnished room upstairs. The Spirit moved in the garden and in the streets. The Spirit of God moved throughout the darkest of nights.

In the moment of betrayal, God took a breath, and the Spirit of God moved. Day one.

In the midst of the darkness of silence, the Spirit of God moved, and God took a breath. Day two.

The darkness gave way to daylight, the Spirit of God moved, and God took a breath. Day three.

On the third day, God exhaled. A stone was rolled away, and God said through the resurrection, "Let there be Light!"

From the night Jesus was betrayed to the morning He arose, the Light of the World shined for all to see. The Light was designed and created to shine in the darkness, in the shadows, in the bleakest of times, in the dreary gloom of the moment.

In a large, furnished room upstairs, in a garden, even in a tomb . . . The Light of Easter cannot be contained.

The Light of the World continues to shine in the darkness.

Letter to the Reader

Dear Reader,

Thank you for taking the time to read *The Night He Was Betrayed*. I pray it helped you look at the night Jesus was betrayed with fresh eyes and a renewed spirit. I hope you've found the light through the darkness as we prepare for Easter. Please consider leaving an online review so that others can discover this pre-Easter Bible study.

Keep an eye out for the next two books in the trilogy.

+ *The Morning He Was Tried*
+ *The Afternoon He Died*

We will walk the treacherous road to Calvary with Jesus. A road of deception and mockery. A road of anger and violence. A road of pain and suffering.

The night of betrayal gave way to the morning He was tried. There were six illegal trials held in a matter of hours. Jesus was treated with cruelty and violence fit for a murderer, not fitting of the Lamb of God. But there was a sacrifice to be made, blood that would be shed, a life that would be given.

We will travel the long and winding road from the garden to the grave. A road that was traveled because of love.

JOHN 15:13 *Greater love has no one than this, that a person will lay down his life for his friends.*

ROMANS 5:8 *But God demonstrates his own love for us in this: While we were still sinners, Christ died for us.*

Sincerely,
Brad Goad

About the Author

Brad Goad was born in Fort Worth, Texas. He graduated from Hardin-Simmons University in Abilene, Texas, before venturing into ministry. After receiving a degree in Bible and Speech Communication, Brad served as a campus minister in New London, Connecticut, at the U.S. Coast Guard Academy and Connecticut College.

He then moved to Calgary, Alberta, Canada, to lead the Winter Games Ministry for Creative Arts for the 1988 Winter Olympics. The ministries in both Connecticut and Canada were with the North American Mission Board.

In 1989, Brad moved to Louisville, Kentucky, to attend seminary and then moved to Nashville, Tennessee, to work at LifeWay Christian Resources. While in Nashville, Brad received a master of business degree from Trevecca Nazarene University. Brad worked with speakers and authors such as Beth Moore, Henry Blackaby, Calvin Miller, John Trent, and Anne Graham Lotz.

In 2004, Brad was called to serve at Second Baptist Church in Houston, Texas. He is pastor of the ministry for adults ages sixty and up on the Woodway Campus.

Brad is married to Rainy, and they have a beautiful daughter, Kamryn, who lives and works in Houston.

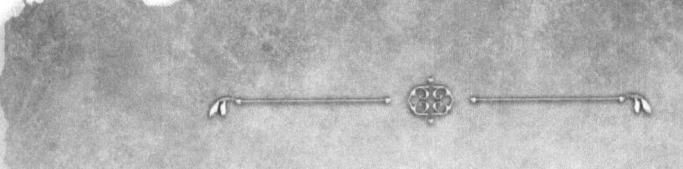

Get the Easter devotional series
for a friend at your favorite
online retailer in paperback or e-book.

Watch for Book Three

The Afternoon He Died

Coming Soon!